Cajun Gumbo
for the
SOUL

Praying for Travelers
on Their Journeys
My Airbnb Experiences

Betsy Comeaux Richard

ISBN 979-8-88540-649-9 (paperback)
ISBN 979-8-89043-588-0 (hardcover)
ISBN 979-8-88540-650-5 (digital)

Christian Faith Publishing
832 Park Avenue
Meadville, PA 16335
www.christianfaithpublishing.com

All proceeds of this book will feed and shelter those experiencing homelessness in Acadiana through Catholic Charities of Acadiana.

Printed in the United States of America

Contents

Foreword

I once had a boss in the travel industry who liked to say: "Travel is a metaphor for life."

This is so true. We are all on a journey. Some of us think we know where we're headed. Some of us know to expect the unexpected. Even those of us with a complete itinerary can find ourselves turned around by God's plans for us.

I spent more than a quarter of a century helping people (in the physical sense) with their journeys at American Airlines, Travelocity, Sabre, and later at the division of General Electric that makes aircraft engines. For me, it was about making the experience better, giving people more chances to get there, and promoting the wonders of travel after 9/11 when few wanted to journey about.

It was business, of course; but my boss and his metaphor-for-life idea, plus a colleague named Liz, reminded me that travel was more than business. These are people. Travel makes their lives fuller. It connects them to the ones they love. It helps them pursue dreams and earn their keep. Let's not forget that, they reminded me. I'm grateful that they both helped me remember this.

In this book, Betsy Richard brings humanity to the many people who are on their physical journeys, and she adds the dimension of the spiritual journey. She brings to life the grandparents, mothers, daughters, those alone on their journeys, and the strangers who we meet on our own journeys and how the journey—both physical and spiritual—can break down barriers. She brings a spirit to all of this that I love.

Wander and wonder.

She got a great glimpse at all of this in the house we both grew up in. Our parents taught us about the power of prayer, with all of us kneeling down each night together and praying as a family. We learned the deep value that prayer brings to our souls and even to our physical health.

We also learned about earthly journeys from our parents, who loaded us up into a motor home on trips that reached Utah and Upstate New York—all six kids, two parents, and occasionally one grandmother.

And then after Betsy bought the house from our parents, she shared this great love for both kinds of journeys with a wide array of people who were on their own journeys. That may be a romantic way to look at an Airbnb that put pictures of my childhood bedroom on the internet, but it rings true in the many stories and people she brings to life in this book.

I hope all who read this book find it enhances all the journeys you are on.

Al Comeaux
Best-selling author of *Change (the) Management*
Brother of Betsy Richard
www.alcomeaux.com

Every book is intended to bring a story for the reader to connect with. This is the case with Betsy Richard's book, *Cajun Gumbo for the Soul: Praying for Travelers on Their Journeys*. Many of us have traveled whether down the street or across the world. Traveling with a welcome from a stranger makes the journey interesting and memorable.

As the owner of BeeBee's 5 Star Best Airbnb, Betsy has welcomed strangers and friends to her home to find a place of rest, whether for a night or for longer periods of time. The experience for the travelers has left lasting memories for Betsy, which she shared thoughtfully through a prayerful lens. The diversity of the guests inspired Betsy to bring their stories to the world through descriptive Scripture passages.

Knowing Betsy all my life (she is one of my first cousins), she has shined like the sun to strangers. Who can deny how special that gift is especially if traveling? This is a unique prayer book for soul-to-soul communication and has led me to reflect on how important compassion is for each of us on the journey of life. For anyone who prays, these stories will lead you to new paths on your journey.

Camille Pavy Claibourne, APRN, PhD
Author of *Dying in God's Hands, Purses and Shoes for Sale*, and *Dog Love and Dog Loss*
Cousin of Betsy Richard
www.Acadianhouse.com

Acknowledgments

I'd like to thank all the travelers and locals who have blessed me with their presence in my upstairs and downstairs rooms at BeeBee's 5 Star Best Airbnb. They are the reason I have written this book. This endeavor brought me so much joy. I am equally grateful to my children: Kayla Moscona, Burton Richard, and Molly Richard. They have always been supportive of my many endeavors. Thanks to Molly for telling me I ought to open an Airbnb and then taking the time to explain what it was. I had no clue! Also, I want to thank my former husband, Carl Richard, for saying yes to opening our home to strangers in October of 2015. After a few guests visited, he said, "You are having so much fun, Betsy. It's like you are on vacation every time a guest arrives!"

x   BETSY COMEAUX RICHARD

Introduction

This prayer book is about praying for strangers. You may find yourself as one of the people in this book. Go ahead, pray for yourself! God encourages us to pray for ourselves as we pray for others. I am grateful for these grace-filled connections and all the experiences that God has allowed me to enjoy through my Airbnb encounters. All of these people have been like the ingredients for an exquisite Cajun gumbo. They have all truly warmed my soul.

Everyone has a story. As I prepared for each guest, I prayed for them, contemplating how their lives might be, asking God to bless them in the way that only he can. I had such great hope that their stay in my "upper rooms" gave them a sense of peace and that their lives were somehow transformed toward him. Hoping that my gestures, smiles, concerns, and hospitality brought a little Cajun warmth to their souls, I continued.

Have you ever pondered 1 Thessalonians 5:17 (ESV), "pray without ceasing"? What a tall command from our Maker and yet one I passionately strive for. In my later years, I find myself praying for strangers and acquaintances more and more…the man walking on the sidewalk of a busy street; the woman juggling three children at the store.

There is a certain internal warmth that arises when praying for others, not knowing their life's world, just praying for what comes to mind and leaving the rest to God. It is all a "God thing" that I enjoy and embrace. It is a small gift I can give to one of God's children, knowing nothing we do goes to waste.

Back in the fall of 2015, one of my precious millennial children, Molly, twin to Burton and younger sister to Kayla, came to our home one day and said, "Mom, you ought to open an Airbnb!" My baby boomer self asked, "What is that?" After she explained and research was done, I talked to my then husband who said, "Well, we can give it a try, and if it doesn't work out, we'll just close it." For over five years, I enjoyed the decision to house travelers on their journeys in the upstairs and downstairs rooms of my home. I experienced a mini-vacation with small glimpses into the lives of travelers from this great nation and abroad.

Growing up in a big family was challenging and fun, especially when vacationing. I wanted my guests to feel comfortable, connected, and cared for. I thought about writing a book about my hosting experiences. A few guests and friends who could tell I loved hosting recommended I do it. I got excited about the idea yet had no idea that it would turn out to be a prayer book. I just followed what came. God placed these unique and special strangers in my life as I became an "empty nester." He has brought me so much joy "for such a time as this" (Esther 4:14 MSG).

Hoping I was of service with the "Martha" in me, I sometimes overdid it. All of these souls have warmed my heart like gumbo warms the soul. Many times, when they left my home, I had tears of joy and sadness; joy since they have expanded my life and sorrow knowing most will never pass this way again. I look to eternity where we may meet again. The gift of prayer is all I had to offer them. The upper room in Acts 1:13 (NIV) is where, after Jesus died, the apostles, Mary, and the women met to pray in fear of the rebellion. It is where some of them saw the risen Christ.

I encourage you to keep your Bible handy or look up the Bible verses as you read these pages!

I have become friends and stayed in touch with many of my guests. Some became "regulars." Some have invited me into their homes.

Those Experiencing Homelessness in the World

Lord, please bless anyone experiencing homelessness with the peace, love, and hope only you can give. Only you know what brought them to this place; however, you told us, "The poor you will always have with you" (Matthew 26:11 NIV). That is so we can help them in our works towards heaven. Please forgive us when we dismiss, ignore, or deny these people of what you would want us to give. Please open our hearts, eyes, ears, hands, and pockets to your call on our lives for them. Whether it be to give our time, talents, treasures, or prayers, help us to have the courage to follow your will in ministry to them. Help us never to take for granted what you have given us and to be always grateful that all our needs are met. Amen.

Everyday Strangers

God Almighty, only you know what strangers' lives are like. Please give them "the peace of God, which surpasses all understanding" (Philippians 4:7 ESV), and a trust and belief that will convert them daily into the likeness of you.

Thank you for the strangers in our lives who give us the opportunity to pray for them. We know that most strangers are just friends we have not met.

Forgive us when we ignore or do not think to be kind or helpful. Amen.

Moms and Daughters

Watching moms and daughters together was so much fun. They loved and agitated each other at the same time. Moms usually allowed the agenda of the daughter to play out. When moms are elderly, it is so refreshing to see daughters care for them in many ways. When there is youth involved, you can tell who runs the household. All in all, traveling together proves love is ever present as blood runs thick.

God Almighty, thank you for the times that bring joy to moms and daughters when they spend time together. These are experiences the Virgin Mary never had. Daughters are a true gift from God. All traits, positive and negative, make their time together special.

Forgive moms when they do not appreciate their daughters and daughters when they forget to thank their moms.

Keep them both in joy and love for each other, give them mutual respect for each other and a depth of caring that words cannot express. Amen.

Dads and Daughters

It brought tears to my eyes when I hosted dads and daughters. They came in all ages, shapes, and personalities, but love was written all over their faces. Some fathers came with young daughters and guided them to watch their step on our back porch and up the treehouse ladders. Others came with their daughters helping *them* to watch their step, kindly returning what they could of the love their father may have given to them as they grew up.

Thank You, Lord, for dads and their daughters. Thank you for the trials they experience and the love so deep they learn from each other.

Forgive all unloving and abusive fathers and daughters.

Bless all fathers with the ability to show their love in a godly manner. Help them to be strong for their daughters until their daughters can be strong for them in return. Bless all daughters with wisdom and acceptance of their dads knowing that the only perfect Father is in heaven. Help them to forgive each other for their trespasses.

As the song by John Mayer says,

> Fathers, be good to your daughters
> Daughters will love like you do
> Girls become lovers who turn into mothers
> So, mothers, be good to your daughters too.

Amen.

Ephesians 6:1–4 (ESV)

Grandparents

Grandparents hold a very special place in many hearts. I happen to be one myself. Some grandparents are spunky and act young for their age. Others need assistance. Most who visited had a great attitude even when they were not with their grandchildren. Statistics show that more and more grandchildren are being raised by their grandparents. One must be sturdy to do that. My mom used to say, "growing old is not for sissies" and "there is a reason God gave babies to younger people." She was right! I admire this group and gain hope from them.

Father in heaven, thank you for grandparents. Thank you for the wisdom they all bring in their unique way.

Father, forgive us when we treat them lesser than the child of God they are.

Give grandparents strength to set boundaries and courage to face the deterioration of their bodies, taking care of themselves all the while. Help them to accept their memory loss and help us to respect and appreciate them. Help us to give them our time. Keep grandparents safe from loneliness and ill-treatment. We pray they live with courage and look forward to eternity with you. Amen.

Children

It warmed this Cajun's soul to see children embracing childhood— playing in the treehouse, swinging on the swings, cuddling and being read to, and being given treats now and then. They are more authentic and transparent than any of us. We can learn so much from them.

Thank you so much for little children. Thank you for allowing children to bring a fresh perspective and wonder to our lives. Thank you for their inquisitiveness and unconditional love.

Forgive us when we disregard the thoughts and feelings of children, for we sometimes forget about their innocence.

Lord, please keep them safe from physical, mental, and spiritual abuse, and safe from the lies of the enemy.

Keep filters over their ears and brightness in their eyes. Give them good caretakers who provide for them through monetary means, actions, and thoughts. Keep them surrounded by your angels, always feeling and knowing your love. Amen.

"Let the little children come to me, and do not hinder them, for the kingdom of God belongs to such as these" (Luke 18:16 NIV).

Personal Family and Kids

I got so excited when I blocked off my rooms in preparation for my family and friends. No matter who they were or where they were coming from, I could not wait to welcome them and share my "upper rooms" with them. There is something about connections, relationships, and love that you just cannot explain when you share your home with loved ones. It's what I had to offer, and I loved offering it.

God Almighty, thank you for family and friends. Thank you for the gift of feeling at home and at peace with all those who visit our homes.

Forgive us when we do not openly give to those we love and who love us.

Bless us with a deeper love and acceptance, caring, and compassion for those we love. Help us to love as you loved and to be and do our best as you would have us be and do. I love you. Amen.

Happily Retired Couples

It is a beautiful thing to observe the love between happily retired couples. The way they accept each other, help each other and listen gives so much hope. Some have idiosyncrasies that could drive some of us bananas, but the unconditional love of a spouse can cancel out all of these. It is so wonderful to watch older married couples work together with one heart, one mind, and one spirit. They smile and ask many questions and do not mind asking for help or telling you what needs to be fixed. Their time is their own, having already passed through the first half of life. They are lovable and loved.

Lord, thank you for the gift of marriage and the couples that have grown old together. Thank you for elderly couples who have kept their strong commitment to their marriage, giving back to you what you gave to them. Thank you for their modeling of honor and respect for each other, sharing in each other's joys and pains.

Keep them strong physically, spiritually, and mentally for each other and their families. When the time comes, place great caregivers in their lives that treat them with love and respect until they rest in peace with you in heaven. Amen.

Philippians 2:1 (NIV)

Young Married Couples or Newlyweds

The joy and enthusiasm my heart received when young couples joined us for a night was unmatched by most. Watching them explore each other and share things neither one may have experienced moved me. They learned, supported, and figured things out together. It brought me so much hope in this morally relaxed age. It was beautiful, new, free, and good.

Father in heaven, thank you for the refreshing feelings a young married couple brings with them on their travels. Thank you for their model of trusting you in making a commitment in this secular world. Thank you for their spontaneity and enthusiasm to spend time together, building their relationship.

Forgive all married couples who forget to love each other the way you want us to love.

Help all married couples trust and turn to you together for everything. Grant them strength, courage, and an unfailing and unconditional love that lasts till "death do us part." Let no man destroy what God brought together. Amen.

Widow(er)s

There is much pain that comes from dealing with the death of a spouse. A very wise friend once told me that "mourning is like a fingerprint, it is different and unique for everyone." One widowed lady stayed for a festival with her friends. They usually attended this festival every year, but the past year, they did not because of her loss. I wondered what it had been like for her the last year, unable to travel due to her saddened state. Two others cried to me and were getting away from all they had been doing daily to take care of the aftermath. You just never know.

Lord Jesus Christ, thank you for the gift of spouses.
Forgive all those who take their spouse for granted.
Please, grant peace and wisdom to all those who have lost a soul mate. Give them joy in the midst of pain. Help them to find support from the community and friends at this challenging time in their lives. Free them from worry about finances and the future. Guide them to look for you, as you are the one and only who will never leave them or forsake them. I love you, Lord. Amen.

Parents and Child Caretakers Who Have Raised Children into Respectful Adults

All of my paying guests were basically good people with manners and respect. Whether they believed in a power greater than themselves or not, they were trained up to be good people. Good manners, respect for human dignity, and politeness were instilled. I have heard many times, "It is not always what is taught but what is caught." We, as parents and caretakers, know it takes an endless number of reminders, corrections, and patience to raise good people who think of others and act in that manner. *Good job and thank you!*

Lord, thank you for your people who teach their children well and are good role models for them. We all know it takes a huge commitment and responsibility. May their tough love permeate respect for all creatures and their Creator.

Forgive us for all the faults we have that have been passed on to our children and for the times we did not treat them as Jesus's parents treated him. Amen.

Families

I have hosted many families, all diverse and unique in their own way. It was a blessing to see how they diligently decided on what to do and when to do it. It is not easy to have everyone's voice heard. But the love and acceptance of all, whether different attitudes exist, is just part of being a family and living in this world.

Lord, thank you for families. Thank you for the commitment on the part of parents to work together to bring life into the world. Thank you for those who do their best to raise their family, helping them set boundaries and treating them and others with respect.

Forgive us, Lord, when we take our families for granted or treat them wrongly.

Please keep families united. Help each member to never be neglected, or abused mentally, physically, or spiritually. May parents be the parents you want them to be. Give each member compassion, acceptance, and understanding for each other. Amen.

College Students and Interns

I've acted as a mom-away-from-home to several young women and men who stayed with me. Internships are intense, exciting, and the finish of long hard work. Interns are ready to begin a new life, and hopefully, a fulfilling job. One young lady became a part of the family, filling a void in the empty nest stage of my life's journey. She cooked, cried, and even watched movies with me. I treated her as one of my own and even brought her to events for my family. She made friends and learned lessons (as I learned from her), and she experienced new joys and struggles. She will be in my heart for as long as I live.

Dear Jesus, thank you for providing people in our lives who are dedicated to the calling you have for them. Help them to take their gifts and assignments you've given them seriously and give them clarity on how important it is for them to know their work inside and out. Help them to recall all they have learned and to finish their studies with flying colors so they can serve your people as you would have them do. When their time comes, usher them into heaven, giving them a pat on the back for a job well done. Amen.

Matthew 25:23 (NIV)

Best Friends

A true friend is priceless. They are someone who mutually and respectfully gives and receives unconditional love. Friends accept and are accepted. Best friends can be honest and loving, expressing every feeling and emotion to each other. They forgive easily, and confidentiality is upheld. They encourage and let live but call each other out on things they know will help them be better people. I know because I have best friends. Many friends that came to our "upper rooms" said it was like a retreat for them, and I bet their relationship with each other deepened.

Dear Lord, thank you for the gift of true friendship. Thank you for the closest thing to your son Jesus we could ever ask for or imagine.

Forgive us when we do not treat friends with the utmost care.

Give all of us the desire to be a trusted and true friend. Help us pick individuals who lift us up and who we can lift up. Ban the enemy from dividing friends. Keep us strong in pure commitment to the relationship. Please bring true friends to those who do not have any. Allow all of us to experience friendship at the deepest level and know that deep love can hurt. Help us to accept that and to love anyway. Lord, show us how to never take friends for granted but to cherish them always. Help us find friends we can share our hearts with, knowing they will accept us, warts and all. Help us to develop, cherish, and respect that friendship. Amen.

John 15:13 (NIV)

Career Travelers

Traveling for work can be fun and exciting, but at times, exhausting and lonely. Many hardworking people who enjoy a change and want to be in a home setting rather than a hotel have chosen Airbnb. It is a way to explore yet be within the comforts of home.

Lord, thank you for our work and careers. Forgive us when we forget the beautiful relationships and the monetary gains our jobs provide for us. Help us to never take for granted making a living.

Keep all those who travel for work safe. Help them to be grateful for this season in their lives. Protect travelers while they are traveling for work, and please keep their families back home safe. Amen.

Ecclesiastes 2:24, 5:20 (NIV)

Colossians 3:23 (NIV)

Teachers and Professors

What would we do without teachers and university professors? Actually, we are all teachers in some aspect. I have heard "it takes a village to raise a child." It is a special calling and a huge responsibility to teach, but more to witness. In this modern age, many times teachers are paid meager wages for these super important jobs. I have hosted retired teachers that continued to voluntarily teach at their churches. I have also hosted new teachers who were ready to take on the world. There were those discouraged by the need and got overwhelmed with the work.

Father in heaven, we thank you that we have teachers and university professors. We thank you that they have answered your call to go forth and enhance the children and young adults of the world.

As one of my friends says, "Help them help you help others." Fill them with your Holy Spirit so they provide your words, thoughts, and actions to those in need. Guide them to direct paths and console their souls. Bless them with patience and wisdom as they embark on their jobs. Keep new teachers from feeling discouraged and seasoned teachers from feeling complacent. Help them embrace their work and easily adjust to change. Have them be your hands and feet.

Lord, thank you for those who embrace higher education for themselves.

Please guide them to weigh the pros and cons of the schools they visit. Direct them to seek not their will, not their parents' will, but your perfect and pleasing will in where, what, and how they choose to study. Grant them scholarships and give them grateful hearts for the opportunities they have available. Let them never take for granted what God has given them in the gift of minds, parents, etc. Help them to make wise decisions with their time and money. Amen.

"Modern man listens more willingly to witnesses than teachers. And if he does listen to teachers, it is because they are witnesses" (Pope Paul VI).

2 Kings 20:3 (NIV)

Deuteronomy 11:19 (NIV)

The Military of the United States of America

There was something that touched, and at the same time, pierced my heart so deeply when I met and greeted military men and women at my home. They were forthright and confident human beings with the utmost of integrity. From telling me that they had the best shower and good night's sleep to being too big for the bed, all of their remarks were transparent. I thought about their lives were like and the scenes and feelings they had to experience. It is frightening. Living in the barracks and on the battlefield takes so much trust, discipline, and love for fellow man. Quietly, I wondered how I had been spared from a calling of this nature.

God our Father, we thank you immensely for those who dedicate their lives to serve the United States of America.

Bless the souls of our military brothers and sisters. They seem to be brave and courageous no matter what they face. Please, oh please, Lord, keep them free from mental and physical illness and from being deprived of their needs when they become veterans. Give them the strength and spirit to come home and adjust easily. Protect them as they protect us. Have them share the ways of teamwork, leadership, and charity they have learned.

Help us to forgive them for any actions that were caused by past trauma. Forgive us when we take them for granted.

Help us to be always grateful for those who give their whole lives to serve and protect us individually and as a country. Keep always on the forefront of our minds and theirs, "In God we trust." Amen.

John 15:13 (NIV)

1 Timothy 2:1–4 (NIV)

Those Young and Away for an Extended Period of Time

So many young people go off to college, take a job far away from home, or for other reasons, leave their family, friends, and familiar culture. Most of them are open and embrace new adventures. They can be excited and lonely at the same time while navigating the new territory. These courageous youth embrace new cultures, weather, and attitudes. Technology saves the day with FaceTime and the likes. I have had many extended stays at BeeBee's Best Airbnb. All of them have been a true blessing.

Dearest compassionate Father, thank you for making humans able to adjust to new experiences. Thanks for giving us the opportunities to spread our wings while experiencing new cultures. Thank you for young adults and their fearlessness to embrace travel and change.

Forgive us when we are not compassionate for those who are lonely and need to talk.

Please give them all safety and "peace that exceeds all understanding" (Philippians 4:7 CEB) when it comes to sadness and loneliness. Help them to appreciate who and what they left behind and never take it for granted. Give them courage and enthusiasm to forge forward with their hopes and dreams. Amen.

Good People with Good Work Ethic

Several men and women stayed with me while on work-related visits. They ranged from cosmetic sales to insulation installers. They valued a quiet place and someone to share their day and their work with. This was their home away from home.

Thank You, Lord, for people with good work ethic. Thank you for providing jobs for them and joy in their lives.

Forgive them when their high expectations set for others are not met.

Protect all workers no matter what they do for a living. Give them what they need mentally, physically, and spiritually to continue until retirement comes. May the living they make provide for the needs of themselves and their families. May they also have time to enjoy the fruits of their labor. Keep them from the temptations of evil in the workplace and on the road. Help them to treat others with dignity and to do the next right thing in all situations. May your angels protect them in all their travels.

Amen.

Those Who Forget Things

I guess that is all of us, right? Travelers have left shirts, towels, sunglasses, cell phones, and someone even left their iPad (they came back for it)! I cannot tell you how many umbrellas and ink pens I have personally left places. Every one of us forgets sometimes, and as we age, it seems to happen more and more. As we say in Cajun country, "C'est la vie!" (That's life!).

Oh, dear God! Thank you that we all can relate to this, and thank you for those who have returned what was taken.

Forgive us when we lash out at family members who have forgotten things. Also, help us to forgive ourselves when we are forgetful.

Please help us to accept that everyone forgets sometimes. Help us to not get frustrated with ourselves when we/they forget. Build honesty into all of us to return things that are not ours.

Amen.

Mark 12:17 (NIV)

Animal Lovers

While I was growing up, my mom claimed to be "allergic" to animals, so we never had true pets. We had a cat that came around, hamsters, and someone gave my sister a rabbit that we had for a while until we gave it away. There have been unwelcomed pets such as the black widows that appeared in the "Among the Oaks" room when my brothers brought branches upstairs. Mom nearly passed out! Needless to say, we didn't allow animals at our Airbnb.

Pets serve such a great purpose to many. They love unconditionally. People feel comfort and love when nothing else can support them. It seems they feel the Spirit of God through this unconditional love. For others, it fills needs and helps people know they are not alone. Many animal lovers have visited. One wonderful couple that visited housed their dog in a dog hotel and could watch their "child" minute by minute from a video on their phone. It brought them peace to know he was okay!

Lord, thank you for animals and the people who care for them. You chose to create pets on this earth to serve a purpose.

Forgive those who do not treat animals with respect and who do not appreciate the blessings that animals have to offer.

May all those who have an unfulfilled need for unconditional love find it in their pets. We pray that all animals are treated with care as you would treat them. Amen.

Sports Fans and Athletes

Sports fans and athletes have stayed in my "upper rooms." They came geared up to play or to support so many kinds of teams. I've had children with their parents stay with me for tournaments. Kids and parents alike asked about TV channels and Wi-Fi, making sure they were ready and prepared to watch the game with no interruptions! Basketball is my favorite sport to watch. During the Final 4 in 2016, the TV upstairs was not working, so a couple with their five-year-old daughter watched the games with me. They had come to town for the Po-Boy Festival.

Lord, thank you for the enthusiasm of athletes and sports fans. Thank you for common bonds that sports develop, bringing together communities and friends.

Forgive those of us who get so wrapped up in the game that we get out of control with our words and actions.

Help sport fans to transfer all that energy, enthusiasm, and excitement into putting you first and spreading your word among the nations. Do not allow sports to consume them in such a way that they become selfish with their time or damage others. Help sports fans and athletes to be mindful of what comes out of their mouths. Keep their mind knowing it is just a game and have them give thanks to you for those who participate. Please keep all their hopes pure with fun and compassion. Disband and disarm any brutality, criticism, curse words, and jealousy from all athletes and fans. Keep them wholesome in their lives and in support of their teams and their rivals. Remind them that we are all one people and help them work towards "being one in spirit and of one mind" (Philippians 2:2 NIV) while "working for the Lord" (Colossians 3:23 NIV). Keep athletes safe from physical harm. Keep their minds and bodies from doing evil things to their opponents. Keep them safe from every kind of addiction. Tame them when they need taming. Keep all athletes and fans close to you as you did King David. Amen.

Musicians

Cajuns are party people who have a passion for music. We find an excuse for festivals and go all out to make visitors welcome and wanting to come back. I have had the privilege of hosting piano players, cellists, band members, guitarists, and more. Music is a gift from God, and those who can sing and play are blessed. I have had young band members and those who played for fun in my backyard tree house. They brought my home to life and filled the place with joy and singing. They were some of the most interesting guests. Many musicians shared their stories and selves freely. Music helps many through difficult times and can soothe many of us.

Thank you, Lord, for music and those who use their gifts for the enjoyment of others as well as themselves. What a wonderful gift of expression you have made for them.

Forgive us when we take for granted this beautiful gift. Also forgive those who create music that is not aligned with your will.

May all those who are gifted with this talent learn to use it wisely and share it with others. May they always bring creativity and freedom to their songs. May they use their gifts to bring praise and glory to you, enjoying what they were given while giving it back to you. Amen.

1 Chronicles 6:31 (NIV)

Travelers from Abroad

When my phone beeped for an international booking, I got tickled inside. It was like vacation for me when I had guests from abroad. They reigned from Australia, Switzerland, Germany, and beyond! I had mostly French and Canadian visitors since many of them wanted to know about where their ancestors settled, who were banned from their country due to religious beliefs. They loved the South. They were so excited about the USA, and many expressed that it is so diverse and welcoming. One group from India said they felt safer and more accepted here than in their own country.

God our Father, thank you for the diversity our brothers and sisters from other lands bring to us. Your cultures are so different all over the world, and we praise and thank you for that.

Forgive us when we demean other cultures and when we are prejudiced.

Keep these travelers safe and joyful. Help them to be awakened to a freedom they can experience only with you. Unite all nations through travelers so that we can live together as one people, your people. Amen.

Job 31:32 (NIV)

Leviticus 19:34 (NIV)

Adventurous Singles

It warmed my heart to host single human beings that had an adventurous spirit. Some lived down the road and just needed to get away for a night or two. Others traveled by themselves due to family and friends not wanting to go or not having funds to travel. They made friends, found out about local cuisine, and kind of just fit right into the family. Only God knows what difficulties they have had.

I give glory and praise to our Lord Jesus Christ for all those who live a single life. Thank you for those who show us an adventurous spirit. Even though they may be very lonely at times, we know they are never alone.

Forgive us if we ever do not show compassion for their individual situations.

Give them joy and courage in all their ways. We pray they feel your presence always and spread their love and self with all. Help them not to just live but to find and embrace their vocation and purpose as you would have it. Let them feel your love and never feel alone. Amen.

Those with No Plan

The traveler with no plan…*I love it!* That is so far from who I am that I cannot imagine showing up somewhere and just enjoying the free flow of the journey. I hosted a couple who purchased an old car for $500 in Canada and traveled until it broke down, wherever that may have been. Another Canadian couple on a tandem rode their bike from New Orleans, a two-and-a-half-hour drive by car, ended up at my home, took the bike apart, shipped it, and flew out behind it. It is incredibly interesting, and for that matter, dangerous! This takes a trust that it will all work out and to let go and live. How beautiful.

Lord, thank you for the travelers who show us you don't always have to have a plan, and everything works out. To "let go and let God" is a grace.

May we all trust in our personal journey where you have us go. Direct our paths. May travelers with no plans inspire us to do the same in our lives…to wake each morning allowing you to plan out our course. Help us to relax and enjoy our journey, knowing you have us in the palm of your hands. Amen.

Jeremiah 29:11 (NIV)

Festival Attendees and Vendors

Lafayette, Louisiana, is the heart of festivals. Travelers from everywhere in the world come to party with us, absorb the culture, and listen to diverse and rich cultural music. They sell, buy, and enjoy the ambiance of our city. It brought me joy to hear them say they loved the festivals and especially that they had a safe, quiet place they could come to at the end of the night. They really loved the hot shower and clean rooms after dancing and kicking up dirt. Some chose to enjoy an evening or morning in the little treehouse in my backyard. Their views on life were uplifting and downright worthy of joy.

Father in heaven, thank you for our festivals and the fun-loving people they bring.

Forgive us when we take for granted the beautiful culture we live in.

Please keep a "festival joy" in our hearts. Help us to spread the love of adventure into other hearts. We ask you to continue to bring joy to visitors all their lives and help them to know it is your joy they experience. Give them wisdom in choosing their lifestyles and friends. May they always find a friend in you. Amen.

Visitors Unmet

There were only a few times when I was not able to meet and greet travelers. It brought out the child in me as I tried to imagine a little about these folks. Face-to-face is my style. My "upper rooms" were just a stop on the journey of their lives, one in the thousands of days they live. Who were they? What were they like? What past affected their present?

Lord, thank you for the movement of your people and how we adjust to different surroundings. Thank you for allowing me to help someone with a pillow for their head and a bed for their body. Thank you for all strangers on their journeys that I will never meet.

Forgive us when we do not offer what we have to others.

Cover visitors with your mercy and grace and never leave their side. Give them hope in you, and may your will be done in their lives. Amen.

Those Who Suffer from Ailments and Society

Many suffer from being bullied due to disabilities, skin diseases, cancer, special needs, autism, and so much more. I always feel blessed when they share. A priest once said as he preached one of his first sermons, "Every human being has one thing for sure in common…suffering." Surely, I have experienced my own suffering and have no idea of the suffering that has taken place in each human being that has rested at my home. I hope suffering was at least temporarily washed away in the "upper rooms" and travelers were comforted. Many people simply suffer due to being unaccepted by others' biases. However, there are those that cause their own pain.

Thank you, God, for suffering. Being grateful for suffering helps us enjoy life even when we are in pain. We suffer with your son, Jesus. Help us to offer our sufferings for others so that our pain has purpose.

Forgive us when we complain about suffering.

God our Savior, keep all our suffering sisters and brothers close to your heart. Give them dignity and give us compassion. Keep them covered with your love. Plant in them an unending joy and acceptance of their reality. Help them to be strong and steadfast in their walk with you. Help them to always feel your presence and know this world is temporary. They will always find rest and acceptance in you. Amen.

"Our heart is restless until it rests in you" (St. Augustine).

The Socially Impaired

Just a few really special people have visited who didn't have the social skills that make it easy to communicate. Either they were reclusive, or they were out of control with their words, actions, and awareness of the world around them. They were usually harmless, with issues and challenges just like we all have. It is just that their challenges are unique and are not always hidden or do not go unrecognized.

Dear Jesus Christ, you have made us in your image, and we are all unique in our own ways. You know the struggles of impaired children and how neglected and ostracized they can be.

Forgive us when we neglect their needs and think less of them.

Please help all those with mental, physical, emotional, and for that matter, spiritual disabilities be accepted and supported by their fellow brothers and sisters. Please give compassion to those of us who encounter them. Help us to love and accept them as your son Jesus showed us to. Let them feel your precious love every minute of every day. Amen.

Psalm 139:13–16 (NIV)

Those Who Give Back

Repeatedly, I was touched by visitors who gave something back, even if they did not know me. There were many beautiful notes, cards, emails, and texts to express gratitude. I received beef jerky, spiced beans, girl scout cookies, Chinese bread, and wall hangings, just to name a few. One of my guests had his wife bring me all the soaps, shampoos, conditioners, and lotions he collected over the years in his hotel travel days for me to use at my Airbnb. The biggest gift of all was the kindness and sharing of God's love. Thoughtfulness goes a long way.

Lord, thank you for the generosity and thoughtfulness of others. Thank you for kind gifts and words.

Forgive us when we were not generous and thoughtful. Have mercy on us for being less generous than you would want us to be.

Pour a special blessing into all those who are prompted to give and do so. Help us to all let go and let you guide our every prompting. Give us the discernment as to what it is you want us to give and the courage to give it. Amen.

The Traveler's Prayer

*In memory of my mom who would gather us to say this
every time we went camping or vacationing:*

May the almighty merciful Lord direct us on our journey. May we maintain in peace and make it prosper. May the Archangel Raphael accompany us on our way and return us to our homes in peace, joy, and health. Amen.

To all Airbnb guests I have had the privilege of hosting, may your life's journey bring you to "upper rooms" again and again as you are guided by God to eternity with him.

About the Author

Betsy Richard is an entrepreneur born and still living in the heart of Cajun Country, Lafayette, Louisiana. She has owned an Airbnb, a direct-selling business, and is now a business consultant and coach owning Betsy Richard Consulting. Betsy is also a certified spiritual director, so she can support many to build a strong(er) relationship with the God of their understanding. She has taught and spoken to thousands for the last forty years on leadership, ethics, and business development among other things. Betsy has participated in prayer partnering for years with women across the nation. Her heart is for Catholic Charities of Acadiana, an organization that feeds and shelters strangers on their journey.

www.betsycrichard.com

www.ingramcontent.com/pod-product-compliance
Lightning Source LLC
Chambersburg PA
CBHW040203160726
48006CB00014B/1874